Synaesthesia

Kylie Huynh

BookLeaf Publishing

India | USA | UK

Presentation by *BookLeaf Publishing*

Web: www.bookleafpub.com

E-mail: info@bookleafpub.com

ISBN: 9789357447461

First edition 2021

Aquamarine

The sandy shore is our past,
each grain of sand
encapsulates a memory.

The rolling waves are our present,
back and forth,
experiencing and feeling.

The horizon is our future
that we hopefully gaze upon in wonder
of what is beyond infinity.

Dreamy Blues

As a child
the world was vivid in my mind
with dreams of flying in the sky
gliding on the surface of oceans and streams
encountering new islands and oases.

Growing up
is like rowing a boat upstream
with rocky starts and rough seas of change
sailing through setbacks
with waves of fear and uncertainty
navigating career and finding meaning
to eventually realising that all along,
they were our childhood dreams
twisted into reality.

Greenery

Lush green patchwork of rice paddies
is seen during summer
autumn brings a brief flash of amber foliage
and the rest of the year,
the world is yellow and brown.

During night-time, starlight speckle the darkness,
emanating a reflection
upon the ripples of the tranquil river.

This place paints a story,
life and death
memories and vision.

Mourning Blue

Childhood adventures, summer vacations
heart and soul of every party
the master of seafood
dried squid, grilled prawns, fresh oysters
sparkling grape wine and fishing trips
wherever you are now,
lingering in the skies or scattered in the blue ocean,
you will always be remembered.

Code Blue

Pain is like an unexpected visitor
knocking at the door
embodying one of many personas:
an archer,
stringing his bow towards the exposed target
a photographer,
capturing wounds and trauma
an educator,
teaching resilience and endurance.

Anchor Grey

It's a strange thing that
even after certain occurrences have happened
no matter how appalling the experience was,
people still go on
eating and drinking
bathing and washing
smiling and laughing
living.

Maybe it's a way of coping,
grounded by reality
or perhaps carrying a burden
in solidarity
to the bottom
of the
sea.

Lamp Black

Days become bright and dim
thoughts turn off and on
but sometimes,
silence can be a beautiful thing
and darkness can be comforting.

Neutral Planet

Sometimes when we stop acting in an automatic way,
we may start to feel sadness and a lack of meaning in
our lives.

These moments are important to stop and reflect
about our lives, our feelings, and our experiences.

Sometimes sadness helps us to seek for our meaning
in life and the meaning is not of rational explaining.

We are deep souls travelling through the universe,
everything is just the way it should be
and we can only truly understand this when we look
from within.

Halcyon Blue

Life can be filled
with the most ecstatic memories.
Yet, also haunted
by the most painful and sorrowful ones.

Fear, grief, loneliness becomes a part of human life,
just like moments of content and euphoria.
Good and bad times.
Successes and failures.

To learn that those halcyon days
families, friendships, memories,
the little things in life should all be cherished.

One chapter in life ends, a rebirth begins.
The cycle repeats and each time,
we will come back stronger and stronger
And to be thankful for all and everything
Life has to offer.

Starry Night

Even when a star is falling,
it will twinkle in the distance
staying with us
in the darkest time and place.

The star shines for everyone in the world,
but in truth, it itself has always been in darkness.

Minimalistic White

Minimalism speaks to us
with a calmer and quieter voice
inviting us to slow down
empty our minds
step away from the treadmill of consumerism
consume less but enjoy more.

It's not about deprivation,
but rather a preference to live with less
to make space to pen a new story –
one of meaningful connections,
experiences,
& self-love.

Mirror Silver

Books are in fact mirrors,
often a reflection of how writers see their worlds
and how it in turn reflects us.

Attitudes are mirrors of the mind.
As our ideas and attitudes evolve across time,
it will mirror the changing values in its depiction.

Books also reflect the side that we don't want to see.
Are we afraid to uncover the unspoken truth?
Why are we reluctant to skip a few pages ahead in
time?

At the same time these written words
binds all perspectives
of the writer, the speaker and us together.
Whichever angle we stand
and wherever we look into,
death, hope, and love unite all of us.

Gatsby Gold

90 years before,
a fairy tale world was invented
but when this world shattered,
it was an illusory reflection
of the failure
of the wealthy American Dream.

'The foul dust that trailed
in the wake of those dreams'
- the violence, destruction, carelessness
a multitude of money becomes a collective madness.

Yet who are we to criticise Gatsby's world
as being tawdry, careless, and immoral?
Do we still value cars, money,
perhaps in search for the Golden Girl
in a white palace?

Still, many of us strive to be Gatsby.

We in some ways,
all dream of moving
up that social ladder
therefore,
Gatsby is us.

Forest Green

The forest is a perplexing place
in myths and fairy tales,
they harbour enemies, demons, villains
it is a place of testing and uncertainty
an unexplored realm full of the unknown
a realm of death bearing the secrets of nature.

Spring Green

I liked the scent of laundry powder,
the one my mother always bought.
It reminded me of spring,
a refreshing cascade,
a garden of frangipanis.

Sometimes, it was a clean fresh smell of sea minerals
a soft blend of bergamot, lemon, and mimosa
crisp marine notes.

The longer we stood by the clothesline,
the stronger and stronger the fragrance was
radiating in short noticeable bursts.

Sunset

The red orb of light falls beneath the landscape
threads of light linger in the sky
mingling with the rolling clouds
dyeing the heavens
amber, orange, and red.

Under the gentle sun,
the sea is an unbroken calm
speckled by fragments of light
each so tiny but together, intense
the sunset is proof that every ending
gives rise to a new beginning.

Coffee

My mornings begin with a coffee,
its rich aroma creating rhythm to my day
sending warmth from the fingertips
to my weary heart.

I tend to gravitate towards the kind
that do not sweeten or dilute themselves
nor mask the bitterness with synthetic sugars.
You know it is just right
when they make you smile, open great conversations,
and make every dull Monday morning
a special moment.

La Vie en Rose

Have you ever glimpsed into rose-coloured lens
and suddenly noticed beauty
in the simplest things:
gentle ocean waves, sunsets, a warm cup of tea,
in a world where roses permeate through the air
with soft music and a warm sunglow,
you remind me that
life will always be
La vie en rose

Chocolate

The key to good chocolate
is not in any single ingredient
it requires:
assembling of shared experiences as the base
contrasted with a dash of personality, order, and taste
then, coated with generous helpings of time and trust
endearing memories together blended,
and gently wrapped with wanderlust.

While chemistry might bring the pieces together,
it's the thought, care, and consistent effort
that all together makes it truly worth it.

Aurora

From black powder to an explosion of hues,
fireworks are seen in many places,
exciting and unpredictable
igniting bright colours into the night
but in reality,
it is rather transitory
existing to mark one of many special happenings.

The scenery I ought to paint is of a different kind –
a sky of pale greens and blues
the beauty of the Aurora Borealis
lighting up the sky in a few fortunate places.

I could boundlessly admire the aurora lights
stretching across the congregation of stars
and beyond the horizon,
this is where I wish
to paint our story.

Curtain Red

When the show is over the sudden silence is brief,
applause ripples and the audience retreats
en masse out the entrance.

The magician clears the stage,
picking up the pieces of his life,
and then prepares to move onto the next show
and while he can stumble upon his deck of cards,
lose his timing and forget,
what magic creates for us
is the beauty for us to believe,
to be fascinated,
to wonder 'why'.

Magic allows us to see vibrant hues
of sunflowers and dandelions
bathed in the tepid air
feeling ourselves lying down
on the dishevelled grass,
erasing all our memories.

In the vibrant colours and vivid scenery,
our mind creates a narrative
orchestrating a vigorous performance
and bringing an empty stage to life.